Things Your Daddy Should Have Taught You

Poetry Written by
Dannie McMillan

World rights reserved. This book or any portion thereof may not be copied or reproduced in any form or manner whatever, except as provided by law, without the written permission of the publisher, except by a reviewer who may quote brief passages in a review.

This book is sold with the understanding that the publisher is not engaged in giving spiritual, legal, medical, or other professional advice. If authoritative advice is needed, the reader should seek the counsel of a competent professional.

Copyright © 2013 Aspect Books
ISBN-13: 978-1-4796-0013-7 (Paperback)
ISBN-13: 978-1-4796-0014-4 (ePub)
ISBN-13: 978-1-4796-0015-1 (Kindle / Mobi)
Library of Congress Control Number: 2013905153

Published by

Acknowledgement

To all who helped make
this project possible,
thank you.

Table of Contents

Acknowledgement iii
Introduction ix
Do You Know What Time It Is? 11
The Story 13
It's a Father's Calling 15
Servant 16
I'm Still Your Daddy 17
Preaching With Power 18
Bought for Love 19
Get Religion 21
Laws 22
The Example 23
The Checkout Line 25
Abraham Obeyed 27
Punk Kid 30
Learn to Do Right 32
God's Got Your Number 34
Acting Up 35
Worldliness 36
Sowing Wild Oats 38
Discreet 39
Wasting Time 40
These Are the Agents of Seduction 41
Gateway Drug 43
Booze Makes Fools 44
Cracked 45
Thanks, Lord, For My Body 46
Fess Up 48
Disgusting 50

Commercial Eyezed 51
Designs by Jesus 53
Proper Attire 54
Mirror, Mirror 55
Playing It Off 57
Christ Has Made Us Free 58
It's Your Life 59
Highway to Hades 60
Ramification of God's Word 61
Golden Delights 62
Treat My Women Right 64
Don't Get Lost in the Sauce 66
Responsible 67
I'm Not a Bad Boy 68
Some Women Remind Me of Creatures 70
Bad Attitude 71
Don't Let Them Dogs Out 73
Blades of Malice 74
Growing in Christ 75
Love One Another 76
No Caste 78
Smile a While 79
Live in the Light 80
I've Got a Pretty Little Sister 82
Why You Want to be a Ho in the House of the Lord 84
Where Have the Five Virgins Gone? 85
Bearing It All 88
Word 89
Be Careful of the Company You Keep 91
Comfort Zone 92
The Law Is Holy 95

Evening News	96
Why should I be concerned?	97
Dreamless	98
Do Right on the Job	101
Admission Requirements	103
Missing Out	105
Who You Creeping Wit	106
Concert of Country Morning	107
Is Anybody Listening	108
Jesus Taught	110
Prepare to Meet Your God	111
No Secret About the Second Coming	112
Obey Your Thirst	113
The Gates	114
When It's All Said and Done	115
Faithful	116
Jesus Says Shine	118
Be One	120
Reviews	121

Introduction

I grew up in Philadelphia in an era of change. There was John F. Kennedy, Martin Luther King Jr., Vietnam, inner-city gang violence, recreational drugs, Black Power, and the hippie movement.

Through all the conflict and positive things of growing up, my dad said one thing that was profound, "If your left eye bothers you, pluck it out." Talk about drastic change! But I knew that it was a figure of speech, meaning don't you let anyone make you do wrong, and don't tolerate your own wrongs, let it go even though it hurts (see Mark 9:43–47).

Well, my dad did not give much more character building advice except do right or else meet the belt. He did not share truths from the Bible because he did not see the value of Bible study and family worship, but every god-respecting man has been given the privilege of being the high priest in his home, to study the divine revelation and to teach his children about their birthright as an adopted son and daughter of the King through the atoning sacrifice of Jesus. For kids whose dad did not share the word in family Bible study, Jesus says come unto me and I will show you the way of life.

Life is all about a chance to change for the better, a metamorphous of the character from ugly to beautiful, from darkness to light, from self to Jesus. It is our job to get ready to go home with Jesus.

Most of my poetry is written in rhythm and rhyme about subjects that affect the character. There's slang and real topics that happen in the "hood," but all are written to help you to keep it real with Jesus.

Dannie McMillan

If the Spirit moves you and you want to step up your relationship with Jesus, please contact www.AmazingFacts.org.

Do You Know What Time It Is?

Sometimes as a kid
While lying in my bed,
A strange feeling would come over me.
It was sort of creepy
Because I wasn't really sleepy,
But I could not move or speak.
When I shouted it went away
Only to return some other day.
What was this bothering me?

I questioned the grown folks.
What they told me was a joke.
They said, "Ah, it's the boogie man; don't be scared.
Just hide under the cover;
He won't know you're there."
I wasn't satisfied with old folk stories and fairy tales.
So when I got older, I blazed a trail,
Seeking to discover the mystery unveil.

What I discovered are some amazing facts,
It's written in the Bible,
But the old folks didn't know that.
They were satisfied with things they had heard,
Never searched for themselves didn't know
God's Word.

Are you satisfied with answers about
things unknown?
Things you've taken for granted,
Truths that have been slanted,
Like a tree that's been planted.

It's time to grow;
You ain't a kid no more.
Not knowing God's Word doesn't make sense,
The truth of the matter that's plain ignorance.
Or are you guilty of indifference.
Lies and traditions are keeping you in submission.
Do you know the real deal about the inquisition?

What does it mean to be saved?
What's going on with folks in the grave?
How high is heaven?
How low is hell?
Do you really know, or you just can't tell?
Don't be blasé
Your own life betray.
Discover for yourself
Then you can say
I know what time it is.

The Story

You know the gospel is for us who fell
It's the story that Jesus came to tell.
It's about breaking off chains,
Jumping off trains bound for hell.

The soul is corrupted,
Disgusted,
Discouraged and busted.
You gotta make a turnaround!
Looking for hope
In order to cope
Pseudo religion is a joke.

Gotta have Jesus
Or nothing at all;
He's the one who breaks the fall.
Listen to His call,
"Come one, come all."
I'm going to my place in outer space
If you want to go with me
You've got to learn to flow with me.

Stop fronting,
Putting on a show with me.
Break free of your vanity.
I'll open your eyes so you can see,
Exercise your will, be still
Stop seeking cheap thrills,
Stop fighting,
Surrender.

Before you have a fender bender,
Wind up maimed,
Wounded and crippled,
I am is not one God—
He's triple.

Knew you before you were a baby
Sucking on a popsicle.
You gotta make a sacrifice;
Don't think twice!

Do it!
I'll get you through it.
Whatever is holding you down,
Don't be a clown,
Give it up for Me
I'll set you free.
We're going to the kingdom!

It's a Father's Calling

It's the father's calling,
Though many of us have fallen,
To be instilling
In our children
The reason for their living.

If the Lord doesn't build the house,
The home won't last;
It's not about trimmed hedges and mowed grass.

It's about time to realize
Children are born to give glory to God
To be channels of righteousness
And live holy lives.

If a child goes unrestrained,
Uncontrolled passions acting insane,
The family and society will suffer;
But dads, it's on us to a large degree.

Servant

I am a servant,
Ain't no shame in the name.
I'll bring it to your table,
Thank God I am able.
I am not a horse in a stable;
I am a man not a label.

Part of the Master's plan,
Jesus gave so that I can,
What will it be?
How can I serve thee?

This is my portion, no distortion.
I am not hiding, just abiding
In Him.

My closest friend,
I would not bow,
He showed me how
When He knelt
With a basin and towel.

I'm Still Your Daddy

She must have felt it did not matter
When she snatched you both away.
Like fallen glass I was shattered,
Broken and betrayed.

Life was much to valuable
To be swept up and thrown away.
So I had to pull myself together,
By the grace of God I stayed.

It was apparent I had drastically been changed;
The pieces did not fit together.
Traces of the glue still remain.
The pictures of the moments when we played
And prayed
Still make me smile.

I am still your daddy, and I love you both the same.
I am sorry for the broken glass,
But the picture still remains.
Sometimes mothers think that
Dad's job is just to earn the bread,
But my heart was bonded to yours,
And my influence was for good.
My heart is still bonded to yours,
And my influence is still for good.

Preaching With Power

Like John the Baptist
From back in the day
Who preached with power,
The crowds were amazed.
It wasn't a joke;
He didn't play with folk.

Preaching and teaching for conviction and decision,
Following after the Savior's vision.
Jesus by night and day,
Taking time to fast and pray;
By beholding John was changed.

The King of glory was his story,
Not about self or no one else.
Repent was the message he sent;
John was determined yeah bent.

On doing God's will,
The kings of earth would threaten to kill,
But fear he didn't swallow that pill.
In these last hours of planet earth,
The message is the same for all it's worth.
Repent and don't be lame,
There's no shame in Jesus' name!
Preach!

Bought for Love

If there's one thing you should know,
Your daddy should have taught you,
It was because of love
That I bought you.
Check it out!

When you went astray,
Because of love I sought you
Sacrificed My life
Was how I bought you.
When you gonna show Me love?
You know you ought to.

Investigate, educate,
Develop your mind so you can relate.
You aim too low so don't expect to grow.
If facts about this world are all you know,

Lessons about blessings,
Giving up the love,
That comes from above.
Talking clean not mean, calm and serene.

The second commandment
Is just like the first,
Talking love
Verse by verse.

Devote your body and mind to My service.
If you do what's right,
There's no need to be nervous.

Stop making yourself the center of attraction;
Your feelings are gonna get hurt by
negative reactions.

Again before I end
I want to remind you,
Show love—it will heal comfort and refine you.

Get Religion

United to be as one
With God the Father, the Holy Spirit, and the Son.

Can you handle it?
You can't.
Dismantle it.
If you push Them away, you're not going to make it.
You can't fake it.
You're imprisoned by bars of self, and you can't break it.

They have the keys of life; reach out and take it.
Old and New Testaments, not one or the other,
Both bring growth.
Follow after truth, say yes, not no;
This is real, not the Truman Show.

When you make the decision to get religion,
Don't leave love out.
It's not about how loud you shout,
What you're wearing so folks can check you out,
Develop faith in His Word, don't doubt.

Laws

You've got physical laws
About bodies in motion,
Force of winds,
Tides in the oceans.
In-laws and relatives of your mom and dad,
Some make you happy, others make you mad.

You've got outlaws like Jesse James,
Folks robbing banks and running street games.

What about God and Jesus, His Son?
The commandment He gave us on the mountain,
Yeah.
We hear all kinds of stories
About how they no longer exist,
Nailed to the cross and dismissed.

Hear this,
If we keep on breaking,
Stealing and taking,
Talking about love, crossing the fingers and faking,
Then an appointment in the lake of fire we
are making.
Wow, that's hot!
Don't want to be in that spot!
Then get right;
Don't fight the truth;
Keep the commandments;
And don't dispute!

The Example

Everybody wants someone to look up to,
An example,
A sample of what's right to do.
Even though
We may not ask,
We are looking for guidance
To deal with the task.

Your mom or dad
May have walked on you,
Leaving no example,
Nothing ample.
Your heart feels trampled, who do you turn to?
Try Jesus,
The Son of God.
From days of eternity by His Father's side,
Made in His image,
No scrimmage.
The love He offers is vintage.

Immanuel,
God with us.
Open up your heart to Him;
Learn to trust.
Merciful,
Gracious,
Abundant in goodness and truth,
All the love He has
It is for you.

You have heard the wages of
sin is sure enough death.
The day is coming when you'll have no breath,
But because of the cross
Where Jesus died,
You can have a place by His side.

In the kingdom
Where the service is love,
Everybody sacrificing,
Serving, and giving,
That's what it's all about,
Real living.

The Checkout Line

I remember so many times
Standing in the checkout line.
Little kids would go off,
Screaming and shaking, jumping and stomping,
Acting possessed.
If it's your child, confess;
Ain't nothing cute, that's a mess!

I've heard it said
Only rotten kids do it,
This ain't true, or is it?

All I know for sure is
My mom didn't play that game.
Begging her for things once she said no,
You were in for trouble in or out the door.
She would give me something to be screaming for—
A whoop, whoop whooping.

My mom was the queen,
And her children were subjects.
When she said go,
It was like turning on the faucet—it was time to flow.
When she said come,
You didn't stand around acting dumb.

Obedience was the word,
Sprout wings and fly like a bird.
While in her nest you did your best,

Until you could fly on your own.
Disrespecting your parents
By a word or an act
Was like jumping in quicksand.
You're going down,
And that's a fact.

We had rules and regulations, and they were enforced.
My sisters and I didn't grow up spoiled;
I am grateful for the discipline and duties my parents gave,
For the love cheerfulness and courteous ways.
My sisters and I were no rug rats,
We obeyed our parents; I thank God for that.

Abraham Obeyed

Abraham obeyed in Genesis 26:5 when God said,
My voice, My statues,
My commandments, and My laws,
This man Abraham heard My call.
When I said go, he did not stall.
The silent influence of his daily life,
The way he taught his children and loved his wife.
Check him out;
That's what I'm talking about.
Benevolence and unselfish courtesy,
The man was upright, admired by kings.
Why?

Because he obeyed Me.
He commanded his household after himself.
There was no sinful neglect to restrain.
The evil of his children
No weak indulgent favoritism.
He did not indulge selfish sentimentalism,
Miscalled love.
They were not allowed to grow up on their own
With undisciplined passions and stubborn wills.
When he said get right, they knew how to chill.
Parents prayerfully listen to the following quotes;
This stuff should leave a lump in your throat.
Don't choke; just change.

Parents' indulgence causes disorder
in families and in society.
It confirms in the young the
desire to follow inclinations
Instead of submitting to the divine requirements.
Thus children grow up with a heart
Adverse to doing God's will.
And they transmit their irreligious,
Insubordinate spirit
To their children's children.
Like Abraham, parents should command their
households after them.

Let obedience to parental
Authority be taught,
And enforced as the first step in
Obedience to the authority of God.

Those who seek to lessen the
claims of God's holy law
Are striking directly at this
foundation of the government.
Families and nations,
Religious parents failing to walk in His statues
Do not command their household
to keep the ways of the Lord.

If the law of God is not made the rule of life,
The children as they make
Homes of their own
Feel under no obligation to teach

Their children what they
Themselves have never been taught.
And this is why there are so many godless families.

Not until parents themselves walk in the laws of the
Lord with perfect hearts
Will they be prepared to command
their children after Them.

A reformation in this respect is needed.
A reformation which shall be deep and broad.

Punk Kid

Mumbling and grumbling,
Fussing and fuming,
Talking out loud to yourself.
Bad attitudes assuming,
Fighting with the neighbors,
Refusing to labor,
Rejecting counsel of your parents is ill behavior.

Lying and stealing and breaking into things,
Lazy, acting crazy chasing folks with sticks.
Teasing and begging,
Accusing folks of not giving
Like you're the only purpose for people living.
Rebellion against your teachers.
Who next the preacher?

You're out of control, and you need to slow down
Before you run up against a brick wall
And get knocked to the ground.
Having to be forced to do your school lessons
You don't believe in counting your blessings.
Putting other kids down is what you do—
This one is ugly, that one is fat;
Poor kid, you just don't know you ain't all that.

Defiant to be corrected even when
you know you're wrong;
You just turn around and sing
that same old song—

I forgot;
Give me another chance!
Kid, you seem to like trouble like
some folks like to dance.
Heart full of hate;
Revengeful and mean;
Except when it's time for the rice and beans.
You want to be bad and look for a fight.
You ought to be thankful for God's protection day
and night.

You're a punk kid looking for attention,
Moaning and groaning,
The point you are missing.
It's time to grow up, chill and listen.

Learn to Do Right

Hey, kid, do you want power
To grow stronger by the hour?
Be like the rangers,
Face up to danger.

I am not talking about might
To do harm, nor strength to do wrong,
But power that God gives to
Stand firm, not just hold on.

If you want it,
It's available to you.
This is what you have to do.
Learn to be wise;
Evil despise.

Spend time with God when you
Open your eyes.
Learn to be just,
Follow God's instructions,
Learn to trust.

Obey the promptings of the Holy Spirit,
Obstacles in your way.
There's power to clear it.
Take time to pray for yourself and others.
Keep the commandments,
Honor father and mother.

Character development is just like muscles—
The more you exercise it the more it grows.
A strong righteous character
Is the only way to go.

God's Got Your Number

I ain't no player hater,
Just a message relayer.
And I want you to know
God's got your number
And it's almost up.
Your sins and iniquities have
Almost filled your cup.

How you think you gonna step to Him
With your homies and childhood friends?
It's one on one, and you're in His court,
Ain't no slam dunking cause this ain't no sport.
Now's the time for confession, or you're going to
come up short.

There ain't going to be no staring Him down,
No getting loud fronting to a crowd,
No whispering, no conspiracies.
No homies to gag, it's going to be bad.
Betta get right now before it's too late.
What God's about to do ain't no fake.

There's ten codes to live by
That would make you tight with Him,
But you can't do them without the Man—
Jesus that's who I am talking about.
Either you're down with Him or you're out.

Acting Up

Adam and Eve had nothing up their sleeve.
When they disobeyed, sin was conceived.
Not the same with us
When we our God distrust.

We can look back through time and see
The results of sin's legacy.
But we want to have our own way.
Most of the time we don't stop to pray;
We just go along like a lamb to the slaughter.
We don't act like sons and daughters
of the most High.

We just go on passing by,
Acting all fly; don't care if we live or die.
It's sad we cause our Savior to cry,
Trying to go higher,
like sly and the Family Stone.
Keep on acting up;
You gonna be skull and bones.

Worldliness

Lust of the flesh;
Lust of the eyes;
Head puffed up and full of pride;
These are the ways of the world.
If you're loving the world,
How can you love God?
Sin + righteousness = a lie.
Inside and out
Shows what you're about.
If you're surfing the Web
And filling your head
With images that cause you to lust,
That's disgusting!

Your heart needs adjusting,
Craving for material things.
You gotta have this,
Gotta have that.
You're a glutton!
If you're poor, you're doubly jacked.
Obsessed with yourself:
How much you know,
How much you own.

You're proud;
Don't say it loud.
If you love God,
You gotta show it.
Craving after the world,
You gonna blow it.

The things of this world
Are gonna pass away.
Confess right now before it's too late.
Follow after righteousness; don't delay.
Kick the world to the curb.

Sowing Wild Oats

You have heard the saying
About sowing wild oats.
You reap what you sow;
You'll get back
What you let go.

Thoughtlessness and ill behavior
Will produce a crop of bad flavor.
You will have to eat your words
And drink your deeds.
So be careful about the seeds
That you sow.

Discreet

Be discreet where you take a seat;
A serpent may lie at your feet.

Blessed is the son who sits not in the
Counsel of the ungodly.
There is no discretion there;
Sometimes it's just about the dollar
And not what's fair.

Be discreet where you take a seat;
A serpent may lie at your feet.

You say it's only a movie, just a flick,
But what is the moral intent behind it?
Does it make you noble or tend to degrade,
Bring glory to God or fallen angels by your side?

Be discreet where you take a seat;
A serpent may lie at your feet.

Wasting Time

Little Jack Horner stood on the corner
    Talking smack and acting all fly,
        Wasting the day;
    In school he should have stayed.
      Now he can barely get by.

These Are the Agents of Seduction

These are the agents of seduction
That confuse youth and bring destruction.

In school they are failing
Because they are inhaling gasoline, paint
thinner, correction fluid, and glue.
After sniffing these fumes, you can't add 2 plus 2.

Amphetamines and stimulants, not just a few,
Diet pills, ecstasy, crank, and ice.
After taking these uppers,
You're racing around like mice.

You're all wired up, now you want to get mellow,
So you drop barbs, rainbows,
Pink ladies, redbirds, and yellows.

Violence and accidents estimated millions of dollars.
What's the number one cause for all this loss?
Alcohol says it all.

Homie, let's get to the point.
If you're looking for real happiness,
It's not in smoking the joint.

About tobacco no need to inform,
Read the surgeon general's label that warns.

Hallucinogens, these will blow your mind,

Make you see ghosts,
Bake your brain like toast.

Window pain, mescaline, PCP, blotter acid
Make you do stupid things like jumping out in traffic.

Cocaine and crack, the cards
against you are stacked.
Takes the fat off your back.
Living a normal life you get jacked,
Doesn't matter if you're white or black.
Takes the money out of your pocket,
Sinks your eyes in their sockets,
All for a high that shoots off like a rocket.

Narcotics go way back when
Folks used to get high in the opium dens.
Heroin, morphine, codeine, or cough medicine;
Living for a nod again and again.

There are many reasons why folks use drugs.
Some are making dollars, but it doesn't make sense.
Get back on track,
Use hope to cope, not dope.

Don't take it light,
Jesus can make it right.
Don't fight, give in.
Make an appointment with Him;
The Healer, not the dealer.

Gateway Drug

Hickory Dickory, Hey Doc!
You sitting around smoking that pot.
Your grades are going to drop.
In school you're going to flop;
Wind up pushing a mop.

An attitude you're going to cop,
Acting a fool you need to stop.
It ain't cool; it's not hip hop.
Drop, drop it like it's hot

Booze Makes Fools

Jack and Jill went up the hill
To buy a fifth of liquor.
Now we know why Jack fell down
And broke his crown
And Jill came tumbling after.

Cracked

Little Miss Muff
Sat on her buff
Rolling a joint one day;
Along came a spider and sat down beside her
And offered her crack cocaine.
She should have got up,
Flicked away that blunt;
But now she's got to pay.

Her life is a mess;
The girl is a whore.
She will knock on your door
For money to buy crack cocaine.

Thanks, Lord, For My Body

Lord, I thank you for this body

My words cannot express,
I am grateful for the lungs that give me breath.
For the face that displays me,
The brain bones and being,
Sockets of my seeing,
Sinews that stretch,
Flanges that catch.

Feet that move me,
Knees that kneel,
Wounds that heal.

Head to toe,
Lord, you know,
You formed me in the womb,
In a sea of plasma.

You opened the gate
Brought me from darkness to meet my fate.
Lord, I thank you for my life,
Help me give my body a living sacrifice.

To eat the foods I should,
To exercise and sweat not to neglect.
To drink clean water, get sunshine and fresh air;
This is how I'll show You I care.

To be temperate in all that I do
Always Lord to trust in You.

And when I lay down early to get my rest,
I'll praise You, Lord, for this great gift.
Amen.

Fess Up

Blessed when God has you covered;
He's got your back.
Don't worry about getting jacked,
But when you are wrong,
You feel you don't belong,
You need to confess,
Get up out of the mess.
You know God sees,
Get down on your knees.
Admit it; get it off your chest.
Go on and get blessed.

All you got to do is to give it up
And get rest.
Seek Him while He may be found;
Find your peace on holy ground.

He will be your hiding place;
Stop denying and seek His face.
He will stick a pin in your troubles,
Bust them up like bubbles,
Give you songs of deliverance.
You know it makes good sense.

He will instruct you and teach you
In the way you should go.
Get up with Jesus and go with the flow.
Don't be like a donkey,
To sin be a flunky.

Get right.
Stop acting like a monkey!
Be a man, take a stand.
You know it's right,
Jesus is the way,
The truth, and the life.

Disgusting

On the net watching porno,
Gonna make you a monkey
Like the chimps in Borneo.
They don't care who they sex;
Don't you realize the spirit is vexed.
Sitting there lusting,
Son, you're disgusting.
Betta ask God for help to do what's right
All the flesh your eyes are consuming,
You're out of control; your soul you're losing.
Corruption and lust will cover you,
It may be too late when someone discovers you.
Get out now, do what you got to do;
Push start and shut down.

Commercial Eyezed

Like Lot in Sodom and Gomorrah,
My dad got us a spot next to the city's borough.
All we could see was the glistening lights,
The towers of Babel scraping the sky.
The poster ad of Gucci and Ralph,
Tommy and Calvin, Nike, wanna be like Mikey,
Polo and FUBU, all reaching in my pockets,
Twisting my perspective out of socket,
Telling me what to do.

I wasn't everyday people, and I wasn't alone.
Yeah my homies and I belonged to the church.
Say hey if you wanna stay,
We just wanna be down with the fashions
So the sistas would be open to our macking.
But you know even though I grew up in the city
And its influence was changing my ways,
I thank God for prayer; I know He cares.

Take me away, Jesus, give me a new start,
Erase this worldliness from my heart.
I want my influence to be on Your side,
Sacrifice like You did. Lord, help me abide.

When I read your Word give me grace to understand.
I don't wanna be a worldly wise man.
Use me, Lord, help me to take a stand.
Help me to share this message with my fellow man.

These fleshly inclinations and selfish demands,
Take them away, Lord, as is Your plan.
Your will, Lord, please not mine.
Thank you, Father,
Hallelujah,
Amen.

Designs by Jesus

The love of God
Who can match it?
If you understood,
You would snatch it.
Get some accessories and flash it.
Spend all your money
If merchants sold it;
Lift it up for eyes to behold it.

Strange thing about me and you,
He gives it freely, and we don't know what to do.
Living in a world of make-believe and pretending
Because your heart is torn and needs mending.
There's only one qualified fit for you,
His love is tailored tried and true.
Put His spirit on,
See what He can do.

When looking in the mirror, you will have to confess,
Designs by Jesus
Brings out the best.

Proper Attire

I was invited to a wedding feast
Among great men in society I am the least.
I was impressed to be among the guest,
So I wanted to look my best.

This one thing I had not expected
To be given a suit from the Groom for this occasion.
I told Him it's OK I have my own.
He said if I am wearing it turn around and go home.

He informed me of the suit He gave
Was to cover my shameful and guilty ways.
The suit He gave had been sanctified
By a life of unfailing obedience and self-denial.

No stains of sin can be seen on it;
I tried it on; it did not fit.
He said that's OK, I will grow into it.
It made me walk with confidence,
Sit with assurance; nothing I owned compared to it.
In Christ I am dressed for the occasion

Mirror, Mirror

Mirror, mirror on the wall,
Do I reflect Jesus at all?
Is there any goodness, mercy, compassion, or love,
Any characteristics that reveal the kingdom above?

Am I humble,
Forbearing, sympathetic, or meek?
Tell me mirror,
Is there any likeness of Jesus you see?

The mirror says,
So you want to be a Christian,
I understand quite well.
You want to go to heaven,
Avoid the fires of hell.

But you are so shallow,
And you don't feel love.
Down to your bones and marrow,
For your sins you don't feel sorrow.
Because you're thinking about doing
The same thing tomorrow.

Cheer up. Want to be a Christian?
There's hope; it's true!
By beholding Jesus
He will change you.

Reading His Word,
Dependent as the birds.
You have to trust in Him;
You don't have power to break from sin.
It's the spirit living in your heart;
He will give you power to do your part.
Little by little imperceptibly,
You will be changed into His image.
Mark my words,
You'll see.

Playing It Off

See you later alligator,
Don't take too long thinking about your Maker.
Playing it off, looking away,
Mixing black and white, you're gonna get gray.
Don't you think it's time to seriously pray?
Partying and drinking, smoking them blunts,
On the day of judgment, who you gonna front?

Jesus ain't about hearing no lies;
Get right or your butt's gonna fry.
You heard your preacher what more can he say?
Trying to share the word,
hoping you would not Stray.

Grow up start drinking from the cup
Gotta learn to walk, not just talk.
Excuses ain't no need,
Got to stop the lust and greed.
That pride you can't hide
Makes you do wrong then turn around and lie;
You ain't sly.

Past the turn styles boarding for heaven.
You won't get by
You gotta ticket, don't flick it,
Get ready, and get with it.

Christ Has Made Us Free

Free!
What it is like
When you have a pain and it goes away
Only to come back again.
How long did it last?
Don't want to bring up the past.
I want to be free, but to what degree?

Not just for a moment
But always.

I know I am sick and in need of a physician;
He tells me to sit down and listen.
I say something is missing.

What no pill, no magic potion?
He says peace be still; I am about to set in motion
A power that will calm your restless emotions.

Here, this is a gift of grace,
Take it each and every day.
The Comforter, He will be with you
To lead you in truth,
But the Bread of Life you must chew.

It's Your Life

If you know better,
Then do better.
Follow what's right
To the letter.
What you make is what you take,
It's your cake,
Don't be half baked.

It's your life, what you gonna do with it?
Are you gonna throw away your chances,
Be a victim of circumstances?

It's your life, what you gonna do with it?
Are you gonna waste away the day,
Stay outside and play?

In the school yard,
Acting all hard,
Your character is marred.
Look it up.
Passions out of control,
Living like a rat in a hole.
Being a bad boy is getting old.
It's your life, what ya gonna do with it?

Highway to Hades

Driving your Mercedes, yeah right you wish.
Plotting on the ladies
You think everybody's crazy or a fool,
Sporting gold and platinum,
Silk and satin.

Paying no attention to the signs,
The music is loud,
And the smoke is blowing your mind.
Strange intersections,
No time for reflection.

No time for God,
You're driving hard.
Homies in the back seat playing cards.
Turning the volume louder,
You're getting prouder with the passing of time.
The sun is setting;
You're running late.
You should have made a U-turn,
But you tempted fate.
Now you're lost on the highway to Hades.

Ramification of God's Word

The Word of God is a powerful prescription,
Helps you break the sin addiction,
Eliminates your words and life contradictions.

Christ and His Word is your obligation;
The study of His Word is true education;
Focus on Jesus and you'll get a duplication.

The Holy Spirit brings about magnification,
Helps you to discern the revelation.

Brings about transformation,
Every day make an application.
This is the way of sanctification,
Which prepares you for the great translation.

Golden Delights

The honeys are sweet
And ready to creep,
Dripping down golden delights at your feet.

They say come and taste as they kiss your face,
But you can't trace the tracks of their tears.
You don't know her burdens, hates, and fears.
Lips she has kissed in hope that disappeared.

Move with caution as you approach her nest,
You move to fast it could be some sticky mess.

A whole lot of sweeties don't know
What they really want.
They're just looking for attention
And somebody to front.

Some want to be mommies,
But they never had a dad,
So they will tend to mistreat you
Because a certain love they never had.

So keep your mind open
While you search for that special one,
Someone with like endeavors,
Sober minded and fun.
When you find the right girl,
Then prize her and treat her right.
Take her to the altar
Then enjoy her golden delights.

Treat My Women Right

Brother, brother,
What's up with you?
Every woman you see
You want to do.

What about your momma?
Would you dog her out,
Dis your sister,
Give her the run-a-round?
Then show some respect for mine,
These women I consider fine.

What is it that you are
Trying to prove?
That yours are better but,
Others abuse.

How would you feel
If the tables were turned?
If your momma was dissed,
And your sister burned?
I am not looking to analyze;
I don't want a compromise.
You're my brother and I don't despise;
Just treat my woman right.

I'll share with you
Like someone shared with me
What it says in Revelation 22:15:
"Dogs will not enter the kingdom of heaven."

If you fear God, then represent.
Fight the urge to chase the cat.
If your left eye bothers you,
Then pluck it out.
Better to enter the kingdom blind
Then not at all.

Don't Get Lost in the Sauce

Don't get lost in the sauce.
Get yourself in a fix in this worldly mix.
You gonna be shaken, ain't no mistaken
Because things are gonna get crazy,
So don't be so lazy.

Get God's Word out;
Read for yourself;
Don't sit around waiting for
everybody else.

Signs of the times are all around,
Killing and stealing and rumors of wars,
False prophets knocking on your doors.
Strange things happening with the seasons,
Religious political movements beyond reason.

These are not smooth sayings;
These words are not pleasing,
But I ain't joking and I ain't teasing.
God is fair it is written there;
He's not trying to take us by surprise,
Just listen up and open your eyes.

Get ready;
Be steady;
Don't be petty;
It's almost time for the confetti—
JESUS IS COMING AGAIN!

Responsible

You better get married boy;
The girl you sleeping with ain't your toy.
She's not a plaything;
She ain't there for your jollies,
Baby acting follies.
She looks for you,
Cooks for you,
Sometimes washes and irons too.
Get a clue!

You know what you need to do.
What you thinking,
You gotta maid,
With no obligation except to get laid?
You're greatly mistaken;
You betta get a job;
Stop being a slob.
Marry the girl, be responsible and provide.

I'm Not a Bad Boy

I am not a bad boy;
I am not a girl's toy.
I've got my mind focused
And my heart is full of joy.

Yeah, I love the pretty women,
And I like to spend the time,
But I should not be giving pleasure to nobody
But my wife.

Before my eyes were opened,
Chasing women was just a game.
But now my hope's on Jesus,
Fornicating is a shame.

I am not a bad boy;
I am not a girl's toy.
I've got my mind focused
And my heart is full of joy.

Sometimes I have slipped,
Lost my balance and fell.
I can't make excuses,
Or I am bound for hell.

It's not easy sometimes making the sacrifice
When the woman is seductive
And seems so nice.
You really, really dig her
And want her for your wife,
But rushing the moment is gonna mess up our life.

Seems out of fashion
To control your sexual passions,
But God's truth is everlasting.
So I gotta take my time,
Get to know her well,
Make sure we're one accord
Before the wedding bells.

Some Women Remind Me of Creatures

Some women remind me of creatures
Like crows in a field.

Taking away, just taking away
Like snakes in the grass, sneaky and creepy.
Saying things behind your back,
Man bashing sessions like a wolf pack.

Like scorpions full of poison just waiting to sting,
They fill their minds with sickening things.
Like rats they feed on the garbage of gossip,
Then bite you to spread their bubonic plaque.

Like black widow spiders waiting for the hour,
Like mad dogs foaming at the mouth,
They just bark and growl, holler and howl,
Act like they're out of their mind.

Is there a pest control for women who have lost it?
If there is a line, some of them have crossed it,
Some are moving to the point of no return.
They have lost the ability to be concerned.
I don't know why,
But I am willing to learn
Why some women act like creatures.[1]

---

[1] Note: If you are interested in overcoming bitterness in your life, read "How to Be Free From Bitterness" by Jim Wilson at www.ccmbooks.org

Bad Attitude

Breaking out your ghetto
Like a sharp stiletto,
Cutting folks down
Don't matter who's around,
Making ugly faces
Angry frowns.

Ain't nobody holding you down
But self.
It's all on you,
Right or wrong.
It's your song, you sang it.
It's your bell, you rang it.
Confess, you like to keep up mess.

Always got to stress,
Don't even act like a lady when wearing a dress,
Tell me what's wrong with acting your best.
If it ain't mean with you, it's just a joke,
Sitting around laughing, busting on folks.
Keep living like that, you gonna have a stroke.
Show some kindness,
Gentle refinement,
Young girl acting like a crooked old
Lady that needs alignment.

Drop the drama,
Meditate on this like a Dalai Lama.
What you sow you're going to reap,
In God's Word you need to peep.
If you're going contrary to His advice,
Change your ways.
Get a life!

Don't Let Them Dogs Out

Is there a solution
For tongue pollution?

Some folks can't make a sentence
Without cussing, sounds like fussing.
It's disgusting;
I ain't trusting
Cuss me out and turn around and say
I was just playing.
No, that's tongue slaying!
If I go to a fountain to get me a drink,
I ain't drinking nothing if the water stinks.

Be consistent; show some resistance.
Don't say everything that flows through your brain.
Put a muzzle on your mouth
If you're going to be lame.

Don't let them dogs out,
Close the gate.
Don't let them nasty words from your lips escape.

Blades of Malice

It takes more to go up
Than to come down.
Sinful relations like gravity
Keeping you around.
With sin don't get cute and cuddly
Like bunny rabbits;
Confess your sins and corrupted habits.

Self-indulgence, pleasure seeking,
Hating, and pride
Gonna make you ugly
It's just not dignified.

It's ridiculous to be so
Envious and jealous;
Chopping folks up in your
Conversations with blades of malice.

Slaughterhouse blood running
All down your blouse;
Tell me who in their right mind
Would want to be your spouse?

Growing in Christ

Sanctify;
Don't go looking for alibis.
Rectify;
Don't deny,
Don't give up before you try.

Truth you say, what's the use?
Folks going to do what they want to do.

You're saved by His Word,
Keep reading and pleading
Until you're succeeding.

The Holy Spirit is like yeast in dough,
Kneading together, oops there you go.
Don't rush, take it slow;
You're going to grow.

Right combination of ingredients,
Like one obedience.
Don't look good?
Don't fret on this; you can bet
Jesus is always ready and set.
It's progressive;
Perfection is made from small successes.

Love One Another

There's nothing weak about being meek (power under
control).
If you gonna be like the Master,
His love is sheik,
Never out of style.
It's what's going on all the time,
From the rising of the sun to the going
Down of the same.
It's the love of God that keeps us,
Make it plain.

Be warm in your heart,
From coldness depart.
Caring for each other is an art;
Paint a bright picture with words and acts;
Let the love of Jesus be a matter of fact.
Christ is the vine, we are the branches.
If we're gonna bear fruit,
Don't be a victim of circumstances.
You say you love God then don't hate
Your sister or brother,
He commands us to love one another.

Get right,
Be children of the Light.
God gave you might
To fight
Against the plight
Of the stronghold of sin
Without and within.
Care for your sisters and brothers,
Be a friend,
Show love to one another.

No Caste

Time is so late,
And we still don't get it.
Acting like the world belongs to us;
Don't want no one else in it.

Setting yourself so high
With your degrees of learning,
Forgot how to use your heart for discerning.

Building up walls
With your money.
Think that cash
Gonna make all your days sunny?

All pride and self-esteem
Don't mean nothing.
Use your talent, develop something.
Humble yourself
Carry the burdens of another.
Ain't no caste with Jesus;
All are sistas and brothas.

Smile a While

I am glad I smiled
And didn't frown.
I'd rather help you up,
Not pull you down.

Your car is in the shop;
Your credit card is maxed.
Refund time is here,
And you ain't getting jack.

I am glad I smiled
And didn't frown.
I'd rather help you up,
Not pull you down.

With the job you're disgusted,
Your "G" can't be trusted.
One day after the eagle flies
You're already busted.

You need props.
Keep on trusting God;
My hope for you won't stop.

I am glad I smiled
And didn't frown.
I'd rather help you up,
Not pull you down.

Live in the Light

Whoever loves his brother lives in the light,
And there is nothing in him to make him
Stumble. 1 John 2:10.

Seeking for defects, calling folks rejects,
Copping an attitude on folks from the projects.
Dwelling on mistakes some small and some great,
Doesn't make a difference
When we don't want to relate.

Sitting up in the church looking like Lurch,
Hating on your brother, treating him like dirt.
Always looking out, never within,
How do we expect to be delivered from sin?
Don't grin it ain't funny; we're going down fast.

Without love we can't last;
Hating is a thing of the past.
Beloved let us love one another
For love is of God
And everyone that loveth is born of God
And knoweth God,
Not just existing and trying to get by.

A new commandment I give unto you
That ye love one another as I have loved you.
That's what I am talking about;
That's doing the do.

In the church we are slacking,
In love we are lacking,
Brothers come in macking,
Sisters styling and distracting.
A little bit of Jesus you know that ain't happening.
Let us get right, live in the light.
Love like Jesus,
And put the devil to flight.

I've Got a Pretty Little Sister

I've got a pretty little sister.
Guys would clock her if she gave them time.
They would stalk her
Until they could rock and roll her, control her mind,
and shape and mold her.

Her romantic flings
Didn't last.
A walk in the park,
A roll in the grass,
Another tear fallen,
Another hope dashed.

Pretty little girl,
When you gonna learn
To get control
So you don't get burned?
Nothing wrong with caring,
Just hold back on body sharing.

When you get so attached
But you're not matched,
Another tear in your heart,
Another guy to patch.

Put on the brakes girl,
Get off the cycle.
It's not about having
Shawn, Edward, and extras like Michael.

You've got skills to develop,
Talents to free,
Hold on girl,
Get your college degree.

I am not saying it's all about schooling,
But self-deception is when yourself you're fooling.

We all know about that biological clock
When time is up we want things right,
But there are some things in life we just can't rush,
No matter how much we put up a fuss.

In the book of Proverbs, Solomon states
There's a time and a place for everything,
Learn to be a queen, girl,
And you will find your King.

Why You Want to be a Ho in the House of the Lord

Man, woman, boy, or girl,
If you are sneaking around
Pulling them down and you're not married,
You are a ho,
Or as the Bible says,
Whore monger.
Don't play ignorant any longer.

You have been given a second chance.
Amend your ways,
Sin, don't romance.
Seek purity of mind, body, and soul;
Reach out until Jesus takes hold.

I can't you say,
No, you just don't want to.
You like doing your own thing,
To fleshly lust you like to cling.
Why you want to be a ho;
You don't care for Christ no mo?

Jesus gave His life
So you can move up.
Don't be corrupt,
Demoralized by sensual eyes.
If your left eye bothers you,
Pluck it out.
Better to enter the kingdom blind than not at all,
Mark 9:43-47.

Where Have the Five Virgins Gone?

I remember the ten,
They were all best friends.
Growing up in the same neighborhood
One thing they had in common—
And the dogs understood—
These women were clean,
You know what I mean.

When they finished their schooling
And mastered their arts,
Whether it was domestic or specialized sort,
They turned their attention to marriage.
Hey what can I say,
I had to give them props.
The girls were about business;
They were not stuck up.

But only five hung around,
And five were gone.
Half of them
No longer sang those church songs.
They sold out somewhere along the way;
They listened to the whispers of the dogs of prey.

The sermons had ceased to admonish them;
Some preachers and deacons wanted them to sin.
Where have the five virgins gone?
One of them is a mother
With a fatherless child,
Another's smoking rocks that come in a vial,
Another's gyrating at some night club.
And, yeah, what's her name is shacking;
She considers marriage no more.

And then there's Mary Jane,
She almost went insane.
Blinded by the world,
Bitter, spiteful, catty, and mean,

But by divine grace
The girl can now see;
She wants to be nice.
Generous, kind, and gracious,
She's trying to get back on track
As a matter of fact.

She asked me to remember her in my prayers.
It's not easy returning to God;
She has to pray awfully hard,
But she's determined by God's grace
To hang in there and run the race;
Someday she hopes to see His face.

As she stands on that sea of glass
With the redeemed nations with forgiven pasts,
Pray for the girl that she will last,
And be faithful to her Father in heaven.

Bearing It All

Tattoo on the small of your back
Directs a gaze to your crack.
Designs brazen on your shoulders
Cause you to dress sassy and bolder.
Down on your ankles there are emblems,
Figures that attract designs that resemble.
Modesty does not become you,
Humility you don't care.

Was it a gag
Or are you a hag?
Seeking to captivate then bag,
Like a black widow spider
With a dazzling shape,
Alluring your victims to your plate.

Think about the markings that you make;
They'll identify you even if you change.

Women dress modestly, with decency and
Subtleness not with braided
hair or gold or pearls or expensive
Clothes, but with good deeds appropriate for
Women who profess to worship God,
1 Timothy 2:9, 10.

Word

Give me the pure and pasteurized milk,
No for synthetic, I want real silk.
Teach me the Word as inspired by God;
Don't dress it up and the truth hide.

I need the real deal;
This old man must be killed.
In order to fulfill God's holy will,
I cannot chill; make it real.
It makes a difference in what I believe,
Hoping in falsehood I am deceived.

If it's right, it's right;
If it's wrong, it's wrong.
Don't give me no bull, I ain't got long.
You better be careful when God's Word you pervert,
It's like dancing with the devil
You'll be screaming at his concert.

Don't flirt with disaster
Follow the will of the Master.
Ain't talking about "P" but "G",
The One who gave you eyes to see.
Grow strong like a tree
Planted by living waters,
Don't just sip, take a dip.
Oh yeah, it's cool and refreshing
For your body and mind.
It's a blessing.

Read it like it is,
Mr. and Miz.
If you want the power that it gives
Word!

Be Careful of the Company You Keep

The influence of your associates can be profound;
If they're not taking you up,
they may be bringing you down
If your eyes are set on heaven and theirs on hell.

Hello,
Does that ring a bell?
Water and oil shaken up does mix,
Testing things blindfolded you may get tricked.
If you're hanging around too long,
you gonna get linked,
What you want a blessing or a curse.
Walking with God you can't be adverse.

Some folks are vicious and ignorant;
Even their mama told them they ain't got no sense.
Your character and reputation are gonna be affected
By the type of friends you have selected.
The counsels of God if rejected
Gonna leave you standing in the rain.

Comfort Zone

Have you been in a space
Where you felt out of place
But you could not trace
The reason why?

You know it's not skin
Cause you fit in.
What?
Too fat,
Too thin,
Come again?

Maybe my style
My nails I didn't file.
I cannot compile.
Too tall,
Too short,
Playing the wrong sports?
Do I look like money,
Or too poor for the honies?
Tell me "G" what's up with me?
I am trying to see
A reason why?
Some folks so fly,
I can't get by.
Some folks so low,
There I don't want to go.

I want to hang around;
Can't find no middle ground.
What is the compromise?
Sometimes I feel despised,
Someone open my eyes.

Help me realize
I ain't trying to be all that.
Just looking for a comfort zone;
Don't want to chill all alone.
Didn't come out
Just to go home.

Hello,
Is anybody out there?
Yeah, some things are so unfair;
Don't seem like nobody cares.
I just want to get out of here.

Some folks don't even want to talk about it.
You chasing that dollar;
Can't even hear your brother holler.

Yeah, This is a trip.
Somewhere I must have slipped,
Fell off in another era.

Folks so cold,
No respect for the old,
Everybody trying to be bold,
Giving you the stare down.

Sistas acting all funny,
Want you to spend all your money.
Don't care 'bout your feelings.
Make a mistake;
They hit the ceiling.

Looking for more out of life;
All you get is strife;
Thank God Jesus made a sacrifice.

The Law Is Holy

In the law, there is no flaw
Makes men stand tall.
Breaking it you begin to fall,
What it offers you can't buy at the mall.

The law is holy,
Just, and good;
Prompts a man to do what he should.

Perversion or conversion,
It's your choice to make.
Walking in God's will you gotta have faith.

Keeping the law
Some say it's hard, yeah grievous,
It makes you sneak around and act mischievous.

It's about love for God and your fellow man.
When the Holy Spirit is in your heart,
You will understand.
Sanctification brings reconciliation,
Getting back to the original plan of creation.
The manifestation of man made in the image of God.

Evening News

The news of crime and corruption,
Political strife, fraud, and sexual seduction.
Killing and stealing, folks going insane,
Constantly in your face day after day
Like a tunnel a funnel taking you down.

With all that mess who can think of heaven?
Christians got to stand for the right,
Fight the good fight,
Be strong and put fear to flight.
Lift up the light in the valley,
Stop living in the alleys.

Cultivate body and mind; be led of the Spirit,
Use your talents, your gifts, skills, and knowledge.

If Jesus has done anything
At all for you,
Then lift Him up so others can get through.

Why should I be concerned?

That ye may be blameless and harmless,
The sons of God,
Without rebuke, in the midst
Of a crooked and perverse Nation,
Among whom ye shine as lights in the world,
Philippians 2:15.

Sometimes I wonder
Why should I be concerned about what others do.
If they don't care for themselves,
Then that's their loss,
They have to pay the cost,
They should have paused longer at the cross.

But I can't help it!
The driving force,
The motivating factor,
Pushing through like a tractor,
Is the spirit of God.

He keeps me coping,
Constantly hoping.
My brother, my sister,
Don't go groping in the darkness of sin.
Come up, come out,
Walk in the light with Him.

Dreamless

I met a girl who never had a dream.
She was pretty,
But at times so mean.
She had no hope,
So in order to cope,
She smoked dope.

She loved to cuss,
Put up a fuss,
Seemed like she did it to amuse us.

I asked her, "Why do you act so hard?"
She replied,
"I've been charred;
You know burned.
So I act like I'm not concerned.
When you live in the projects,
Folks treat you like rejects,
So you try to protect
The little space you have until you can eject.
Can you relate to that?"

I told her, "Yeah, I am down;
I have been around,
Grew up in the hood.
I understood."

But there comes a time for change.
We cannot remain insane;

We put God to shame.
She said make it plain,
So I gave her a poem,
And this is what it said.

If there's one thing you should know,
Your daddy should have taught you.
It was because of love that Jesus bought you;
Check it out!

When you went astray
Because of love that He sought you,
Sacrificed His life
Was how He bought you.

When you gonna show Him love?
You know you ought to.
Investigate, educate;
Develop your mind so you can relate.

You aim too low so don't expect to grow.
If facts about this world is all you know,
Lessons about blessings,
Giving up the love
That comes from above.

Talking clean, not mean, calm and serene.
The second commandment is just like the first,
Talking love
Verse by verse.
Devote your body and mind to His service;

Do what's right,
No need to be nervous.

Stop making yourself the center of attraction;
Your feelings gonna get hurt by negative reactions.

Again,
Before I end,
I want to remind you,
Show love.
It will heal,
Strengthen,
And refine you.

Do Right on the Job

Folks gonna treat you bad every now and then,
Stab you in the back,
In the front they're your friend.
Make you want to get up from your job and quit,
But don't you worry;
Don't be in a hurry to make them do right;
God is watching, He sees your plight.
The race is not to the swift,
No not to the strong,
But those who trust in Jesus and hold on.

You have got to understand
That's what God demands;
You must be patient and follow His plan.
Show love to everybody you know,
Even the ones who don't want you to grow.
It's about caring,
Praying for your enemies and their burdens sharing.

It's not a game you learn to play,
Too bad it's just not that way.
Don't be a phony,
Or you might as well get out of Dodge on your wooden pony.
On the job people act like slobs,
Treat you so bad
You think you're dealing with the mob.
Hey you gotta earn your money,
Even if folks are acting all funny.

Holdout,
Maybe one more round before you win the bout'.
Then you can shout,
Hallelujah!
Thank you Lord for showing me the way,
To earn my money one more day.

Admission Requirements

The Ten Commandments,
They're not a catalog of college electives.
It's not pick and choose nor be selective;
They're not ten top suggestions by the faculty.
If you don't know,
Check out a Bible from the library.

You do the math,
—10=10—
Nothing taken out,
Nothing put in.

It shouldn't take a course in
rocket science to figure them out,
Keep it plain and simple,
that's what God is talking about.
Love for God and your fellow human beings,
Come on people let's do this thing.

Ecclesiastes makes it plain,
Fear God and keep
His commandments
Otherwise
There will be no admission to His kingdom
Because you won't be graduating from the earth.
Oh by the way,
There's only so many days
left to put them into practice,
Then the class will be dropped,
And there will be NO REFUNDS!

Missing Out

Seeking
Associate's degrees,
Bachelor's degrees,
Then your master's.
So focused on what you're doing,
You don't see the coming disaster.

With visions of money making in your head,
First thing in the morning until it's time for bed.
Generation X gadget consumers,
Just like the former baby boomers.

Don't you know, haven't you heard?
Seek ye first the kingdom of God,
He knows your needs and will provide.

You are so concerned with how you dress,
Head in the clouds stepping toward the mess.
You have an adversary from way back when,
He's smiling at you, but he's not your friend.
He's your enemy and that's his devilish grin.

He will chew you up like an apple,
Drink you down like Snapple,
Without the seal of God, nothing's ample.
Don't get tripped, fall and stumble,
Missing out on heaven is the greatest fumble.

Who You Creeping Wit

Who you creeping wit?
Who you sleeping wit?

If your mama knew, she would have a fit.
Sent you to school to get an education,
You running around having sexual relations.

Who you creeping wit?
Who you sleeping wit?

Them brothers wearing gold
Are turning your head.
Next thing you know you're
Sleeping in their beds.

The rhythm and rhyme
Is blowing your mind.
For religious things you
Don't have much time.

Who you creeping wit?
Who you sleeping wit?

Are you so desperate you can't wait?
Betta find a husband then relate.

Who you creeping wit?
Who you sleeping wit?

Concert of Country Morning

Loyal as the sun that rises,
True as the appointment of the moon,
God is waiting for us.

Crisp is the morning air,
Filled with melodies fair,
Birds, crickets, tree frogs, and the crow of roosters,
Awake from your slumber and seek Him.
With gratitude greet Him,
Open His Word,
And drink from the life giving fountain.

Welcome to this sacred hour,
The concert of country morning.

Is Anybody Listening

Hello,
Is anybody listening anymore?
Pick me up,
Open me,
Take a look inside.
Ponder me,
Be glad.
Let your heart break,
Be sad,
Get mad.

Don't put me down so quickly,
Stay a while longer.
Sing with me,
Cry with me,
Don't misconstrue and lie on me.

I can change your mind,
You need to rely on me.
I've been around for a long, long time;
Faith you got to have to confide in me;
Generations have been inspired by me.
Hold me close,
Let your heart pound.
Aren't you grateful that I'm around?
Love me,
Cherish me.

Multitudes have died for me,
Follow me in your words and actions.
I'll teach you,
I know how to reach you,
Just pick me up and stay awhile.
Yours truly,
Forever,
Day by day,
Biblios
P.S.
Pray for discernment first!

Jesus Taught

Out on the mountaintops,
In the fields of green,
Jesus taught the multitudes
And healed their diseases.

He came to give peace,
And from their burdens release,
Showed them the way to heaven
If from sin they would cease.

Come unto me
All ye who are burdened and in need of rest,
Spend time in my Word,
And you will be blessed.

Prepare to Meet Your God

Bolts of lighting,
The thunders frightening.
Adrenalin rushing through your brain.

Time refrains,
What is
Won't last
Like a blast
It's gone.
No more song,
No more dance,
No lips to kiss,
No engaging romance.

Time how you use it,
Determines your future.
The moments are fleeting,
Wasted time is depleting.

Jesus is coming down,
Will you be going up?
Lay that love novel to the side.

Time to recognize what you should prioritize;
Prepare to meet your God.

No Secret About the Second Coming

Don't want to be a prophet of doom,
But Jesus Christ is coming soon.
May be morning, may be noon,
It don't matter when the earth goes BOOM!!!!

That's right, won't be no secret when He comes back;
The second coming He ain't cutting no slack.
If you're not changed in that moment, then you
gonna be jacked.
Righteous dead popping up out of the graves;
The righteous living have got it made.

But the wicked living,
Weeping and wailing and gnashing of teeth.
They have sold out by following the beast,
And there time shall be no more.

But that's not all folks;
It's not over yet.
There's more to this drama
On this you can bet.
If you know the facts,
Hopefully you won't regret;
Revelation 22:10–21.

Obey Your Thirst

The women at the well
Had been living in a desert
Reserved for hell.

Deceived by notions of her sensual emotions
Until she obeyed her thirst.

Jesus offered her water
From wells that never run dry.

Living streams that quench the thirst of every
Soul's deepest desire;
Gatorade for a marathon, decathlons, and sprints,
But Christ gives the water of His Holy Spirit.

We are all searching for that special fountain
That will satisfy our dying soul,
Keep us young,
Full of fun,
Give us power to run this race of life,
Deal with ease, less stress, and strife.

Then obey your thirst,
Jesus, Water of Life.

The Gates

No dogs,
No cats,
No getting over like fat rats.
No pigs,
No chickens,
No snakes in the grass.
Nothing that defiles will get past
The gates to the kingdom of heaven.

If you hope to go there,
Now's the time to prepare.
Can't be careless,
Manners a mess,
Confess.

Your language is tasteless,
Give Christ your heart.
Do your part,
Choose to clean up those ugly thoughts.
Not just talking 'bout lust,
But trust.
Deep in your soul,
Is it warm or freezing cold?
Proud, selfish, and greedy, you know you're needy.
No transformation,
No transportation,
To the kingdom.

When It's All Said and Done

When it's all been said and done
Where have the moments gone?
Our words and actions have they gone astray,
Caused confusion hurt and pain?

Have they bashed a man upside his head,
Falsely labeled a woman you really don't know,
Stunted the child that was trying to grow?
You feel good when you have had the last word,
But the last word you haven't yet heard.

On this you can bet
That by your words and your actions
You will be justified or condemned.
A word of advice as from a friend,
Weigh what you say before it is said,
Don't lay no heavies on your neighbor's head.

There is a book of remembrance
For everything you say and do
After it is all said and done.

Faithful

Watch out! Be careful! Don't you dare!
Some folks don't care.
They will burn you like a flare;
In bewilderment you will stare.

There are those who will impose,
Take away your portion on tippy toes.
They look like your brother, but it's another;
He's a scoffer with nothing to offer
But deceit and lies.

He won't deny that the Lord is coming,
But getting ready he's not trying.
When you try to do your best,
He says take a rest.
Some things you can guess,
Take the world as your portion,
Beg, borrow, or extortion.

Peace and safety,
We've got it made
In the shade
Sipping on lemonade.
We are out to get paid;
Let us party, join the parade.

Meanwhile, all of a sudden
Like a thief in the night
There He is in your face,
Jesus Christ,
With no more grace.

You wish you were in another place;
The player got played;
The greedy got paid.
Oh no! You're not making the grade.
You wish you had stayed
Faithful.

Jesus Says Shine

Shine, shine
If you are mine;
Don't compromise with darkness,
Don't play blind.

I am the great light,
Bright like the sun.
You are my stars;
Without me you ain't got none.

The world is dark,
Lying in sin.
Don't turn away from Me,
Because of a friend.

You know your thoughts,
Purposes, and motives I read;
My light reveals your darkness indeed.
Represent,
Glow,
Let your light show.
Reveal My grace and My power,
Tell the world I am the Man of the hour.

It's about Me,
Not you.
Let My light shine through.
I am about making the impossible come true,
I'm your sick hearts remedy.
As long as you stay in step with me,
I am your Redeemer,
The cleaner ain't no misdemeanor.

I'm talking serious;
This is not delirious.
Don't walk on Me because of trials and reproach,
Hiding in dark corners like a little roach.

Listen to the word,
Do what you heard.
It's a lamp to your feet,
A light for your path.
Trust in me,
I am precise like math.
I have come to redeem you from your dark past,
SO SHINE!

Be One

Now I am no more in the world but these
Are in the world and I come to thee
Holy Father keep through Thy own name
Those whom Thou hast given Me that they
May be one as We are. John 17:11.

No solos, no anything goes, no one man shows,
Without the seed nothing grows.
A man and a woman equal two,
Place them together see what they do.
Are they gonna be true
To the calling God gives?
Living together to be united as one,
Overcoming that pride and selfishness,
It's my way or none.

It's got to be like the Father and the Son,
Working in harmony to get things done.
There's more to a home than living in it;
It's a place where angels should love to visit,
Where the Word of God is opened and cherished,
Where respect is shown and bad attitudes banished.

Sanctification is what we need,
Not following the flesh distrust and greed.
To come into harmony with God's plan,
Is why the Holy Spirit was given to man.

Reviews

"This volume is an outstanding tool that can be used to help young people explore positive solutions to very real problems they are facing ... this is in line with the principles in Philippians 4:8 ... highly motivational to anyone seeking a closer walk with the Lord ... it is pregnant with old ideas put in modern day, creative language ... that will entertain and inspire young and old alike."

—Pastor William Smith,
Oakwood College literature evangelist director

"One of the best accumulations of spirituality poetic expressions I've ever read. His poems are filled with truth, depth, sincerity, concern, and above all REALITY ... captivates the young ... offers a lesson in life ... good reading for older generations."

—Betty J. Batts,
business woman, entrepreneur

"Sit back with your heart wide open. This volume will jolt you into reality and entice your senses. It's the real world without rose colored glasses."

—Dion Taylor,
student

To purchase copies of my book or schedule appointments for guest appearances, please contact me at **DannieMcMillan@ASPECTBooks.com**.

We invite you to view the complete
selection of titles we publish at:

www.AspectBooks.com

Scan with your mobile
device to go directly
to our website.

Please write or email us your praises, reactions, or
thoughts about this or any other book we publish at:

P.O. Box 954
Ringgold, GA 30736

info@AspectBooks.com

Aspect Books titles may be purchased in bulk for
educational, business, fund-raising, or sales promotional use.
For information, please e-mail

BulkSales@AspectBooks.com

Finally, if you are interested in seeing
your own book in print, please contact us at

publishing@AspectBooks.com

We would be happy to review your manuscript for free.